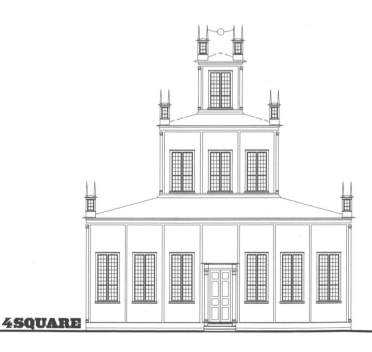

4SQUARE

4SQUARE

An introduction to the Sharon Temple National Historic Site, to the Children of Peace who made it, and to their place in the history of Canada before Canada

*Mark Fram &
Albert Schrauwers*

Coach House Books

2005

Acknowledgements

Over the years that we both have been advisers and volunteers, and occasionally governors, of the Sharon Temple site, we have both worked with many good people who have shared the daunting task of keeping the buildings, collections and site in proper order for the future. There are far too many to mention in total, but we absolutely must single out our deep appreciation for Ruth Haines – for many years the site's curator, director and general caregiver – who, perhaps more than anyone, made us each feel so inordinately and personally responsible for the place that we finally had to produce this little book, since no one else had ever gotten around to it. Till now.

The authors thank Steven Evans for permission to reproduce from his collection the rare historic stereoscopic view on page 28 and the details on pages 44–5. We also thank Gary Evans for the results of his patient re-photographing of the Temple through every season. We gleaned maps and many of the more ancient illustrations from the vast pictorial resources at the libraries of the University of Toronto, and particularly acknowledge the help of Marcel Fortin, GIS & Map Librarian. Otherwise, the bulk of the historical pictures are from the Sharon Temple Museum Society's collections, and the modern-day photographs from Mark Fram.

We are tremendously grateful for the researches and publications of W. John McIntyre, a long-time friend of the Temple, from whose book *Children of Peace* (McGill-Queen's University Press, 1994) we have borrowed, with thanks, and to which we commend readers who wish to seek out more detail. His book complements Albert Schrauwers, *Awaiting the Millennium: The Children of Peace and the Village of Hope, 1812–1889* (University of Toronto Press, 1993).

And, of course, not at all least, our thanks to Stan Bevington, and the Coach House cabal, as editors, publishers, printers and friends of the Temple, too.

Library and Archives Canada Cataloguing in Publication

Fram, Mark
    Foursquare : an introduction to the Sharon Temple National Historic Site / Mark Fram, Albert Schrauwers.

ISBN 1-55245-164-x

    1. Sharon Temple National Historic Site of Canada (Sharon, Ont.) 2. Historic sites—Ontario—Sharon. I. Schrauwers, Albert II. Title.

FC3064.S53F73 2005   971.3′547   C2005-903420-3

Prelude and overture

A skyline dominated by a structure intended for worship is not an unusual feature anywhere in the world. But this Temple is more unusual than most. Chief among its peculiarities is what gives this slim volume its title: the building is precisely *foursquare*, with four identical and fully symmetrical elevations, down to the smallest detail, all on a square plan. Indeed, that square plan is made up of squares within squares, from an exquisitely grand picket fence with four gates, through four sets of double doors, into a terraced chamber at whose centre sits – surprise! – a little foursquare building with four identical, symmetrical windowed faces and four pairs of little doors that open into a little chamber at whose centre sits a square table, on which rests an open book.

The book lies open at the intersection of the primary lines or axes of symmetry of the Temple. At a much larger scale, the Temple sits at the intersection of two axes of history – a commonplace local society of the early 19th century in Upper Canada, intersecting a three-thousand-year struggle to recover a myth of a paradise lost, a dream of heaven on earth, a perfect place in an imperfect world. This Temple is far from a "merely" religious building.

Contrary to conventional wisdom about small religious and communitarian groups in the 19th century, the builders and occupants of the Temple – the Children of Peace, whom you will get to know shortly – were not at all an isolated, defensive, world-fearing sect, detached from the early settlement and events of what is now southern Ontario. If anything, this group was the complete opposite of "hermetic." The un-shy and non-retiring Children of Peace have attracted attention since their founding before 1820. Their Temple, one of several meeting houses and accessory buildings they built and occupied from the 1810s until the 1880s, was noted and publicized as a splendid architectural curiosity even while it was under construction in the late 1820s. And even though they disappeared as an organized group well before 1900, they continued then and continue still to attract curiosity.

This little book aims to satisfy some of that curiosity, and at the same time to pique it a good deal further.

This is a guide for two kinds of audience — both the visitor to the place and everyone else. For those who have been able to visit and see the Temple inside and out, together with its surrounding landscape, buildings and artifacts, this book is a retrospective guide, with information you might have heard, or not, and ideas and views that you might have remembered, or not. For those who have not (yet) seen the place, this is both an invitation to come see for yourself, and a nudge, of a more general kind, to explore other historic places and stories nearby in both geography and history.

As to why this page is a "prelude and overture" rather than a mere "preface," it should become clear that the Children of Peace were, among many other distinctions, more than a little musical.

Contents

The plan of the book and, not coincidentally, the Temple

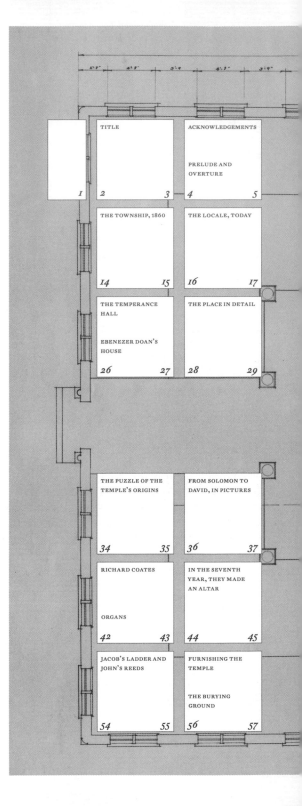

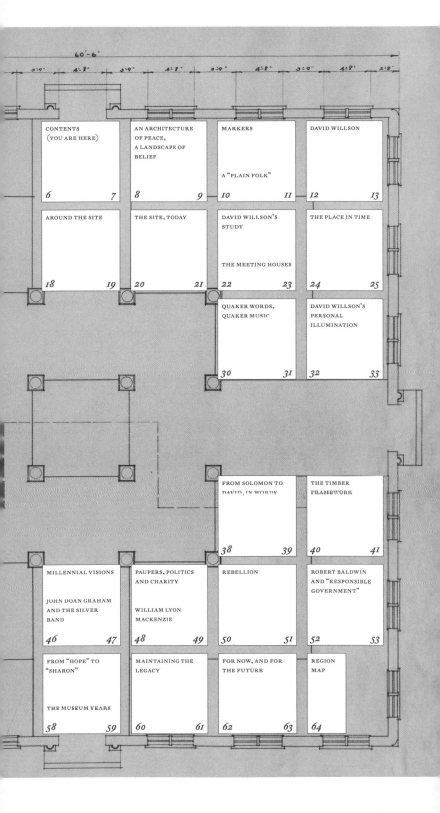

An architecture of peace,
a landscape of belief

In their first three decades, the members of the Children of Peace erected buildings for both worship and communal activity along the street frontage of David Willson's farm. The most notable, both then and now, is the Temple of Peace, constructed under the direction of master builder Ebenezer Doan over an extended period from 1825 to 1831 and dedicated in 1832. Based on Willson's visions, and drawn from his concept of reconciliation of Old and New Testament sources, the Temple was the most conspicuous architectural embodiment of the beliefs and practices of the Children of Peace.

The Temple was not a church or an active centre of weekly worship. It was reserved for meetings and the collection of alms on the last Saturday of each month, for special feasts on "June Day" and at the Illumination in September, and for a Christmas worship meeting. Weekly meetings for worship in the Quaker fashion were held in one of two meeting houses, now vanished, just south of the site.

The Temple is a fully symmetrical foursquare construction comprising three tiers from a sixty-foot-square base to a twelve-foot-square architectural lantern. Each tier is faced with paired multi-paned windows on all four sides, and at each of the twelve corners of the roof is a small lantern of square plan, with its own four corners accented by a gilded spikes. The twelve corner lanterns, together with every window on all three levels, were lit once a year at the Illumination, to represent the shining forth of the "light of God" into the world.

According to David Willson, "in his own words as the writer [Emily McArthur, recollecting in 1898] heard him repeat it,"

My meaning for the three stories is to represent the Trinity. Being square at base meant to deal on the square with all people. The door in the centre on each

8

of the four sides is to let the people come in from the east and the west, the north and the south on equal and the same footing. The equal number of windows on each side of every door is to let the light of the gospel be equally the same on all the people assembled herein. The four pillars at each corner of the Altar, with the words Faith, Hope Love and Charity inscribed on them is [sic] the four cardinal virtues which are the foundation or in other words the principles upon which it is built. The Golden Ball on the top storey with the word "peace" inscribed meant peace to the world.

At the centre of the interior, approachable equally from the four doorways and illuminated by indirect light in the central three-storey well, is the Altar, or Ark – a foursquare building-in-miniature displaying inside a Bible open at the Ten Commandments (as well as manuscripts concealed within at the building's dedication in 1832 and rediscovered during restoration in the early 1990s). The upper-storey musicians' gallery – from which the players can be heard but not seen – is reached by a carefully bowed staircase traditionally known as "Jacob's Ladder."

Though the Temple stood slightly back from the village street inside a small square compound defined by an architectural fence corresponding to the style of the building, the entire complex was tightly integrated with the village itself. This remarkable structure was not a church; it was and it remains a great deal more than a church. Inspired by biblical visions and remembrances of the first Temple of the Israelites, following a centuries-old tradition that sought to re-establish a divine presence and a world of peace in architectural form, and incorporating their own sense of social justice and faith in their own lives, the Children of Peace created and left behind a legacy whose most conspicuous building may be as close to perfection as humankind can ever hope to make.

Markers

SHARON TEMPLE

This elegant structure stands as testament to the faith and good works of the Children of Peace. In 1825–1832 master carpenters Ebenezer and John Doan constructed it to the plans of religious leader David Willson who was inspired by Biblical descriptions of Solomon's Temple and the New Jerusalem. The square plan symbolized the sect's egalitarian beliefs and co-operative principles. Once a month and on holidays the Temple was the scene of music-filled ceremonies. Its rescue from demolition in 1918 by the York Pioneer and Historical Society is an early example of historic conservation in Canada.

> Historic Sites and Monuments Board of Canada
> Government of Canada

SHARON TEMPLE

Erected 1825–32, its architecture symbolizes the religious beliefs of its builder, David Willson, born in New York State 1778. Disowned by the Society of Friends (Quakers), he established hereabouts the Children of Peace (Davidites) in 1812, a small sect which retained some Quaker mysticism while placing great emphasis on ceremony, music and practical education. Most Davidites were strong political reformers and several joined Mackenzie's force in the Rebellion of 1837. Following Willson's death 1866, the strength of the sect diminished, and its last service was held here 1886.

> Erected by the Ontario Archaeological and
> Historic Sites Board.

(UNTITLED)

He [David Willson] has given gratis to his brethren his services as a builder, also the ground whereon our three buildings of worship stand. And although he is a man not versed in science, yet his pattern for building will stand the test of the most strict scrutiny, and we can say the house (which he designed) for our monthly sacrifice has obtained the character of being a modern structure for chasteness of design unsurpassed.

> John and Ebenezer Doan
> (Postscript to David Willson's book, *The Impressions of the Mind,* Toronto, 1835)

In 1801, members of the Society of Friends – who would soon become the Children of Peace – began to arrive in York County from Pennsylvania and Vermont. Better known as the Quakers, they were a "plain folk" (not unlike the Mennonites and Amish), eschewing all religious and personal ornamentation. During the War of Independence they had maintained their pacifist doctrine, and many revolutionaries had construed that pacifism to be support for the British. Many Quakers came to Upper Canada in search of free land and an escape from religious persecution in the new American republic. It is a particular irony that this plain folk should produce one of the most colourful congregations in Ontario's history.

A "plain folk"

Among these early settlers was David Willson of New York State, who took up land in East Gwillimbury township. Many of Willson's relatives, including the Dunham, Reid and Briggs families, came to settle nearby as well. They established a small community of spirit rather than an actual village: a cluster of farms in the neighbourhood of their meeting house, built in 1810 on land near Yonge Street donated by Willson. Here, twice a week, the local Quakers came to meet and worship. The original meeting house, the first church in the township, still survives. ⟶

Quakers do not have an ordained clergy – those Friends who feel led by the spirit of God to speak will spontaneously stand to preach in worship meetings. After David Willson stood to preach at a Yonge Street Monthly Meeting in 1811, a small segment of the assembly received his ministry rather poorly: "Mary [Pearson] asked [Willson's] wife if she had discovered something of her husbands being out of his right mind."

Willson was accused of heresy, of denying the divinity of Christ, and of deism – charges which he then spent great energy refuting, and then doing something quite different altogether.

David Willson

Theologian, poet, hymnodist and political reformer David Willson was born June 7, 1778, in the Nine Partners Grant of Dutchess County, New York, son of John and Catherine Willson, "poor but pious Presbyterians ... whose fortune in life left me far below the means of common school-learning." David's father died when he was fourteen, at which time David apprenticed to a carpenter.

In 1798, David's elder brother Hugh moved the family to New York City with their new brides, sisters Phebe and Mary Titus, daughters of a Quaker minister. They bought a share in a sloop, *The Farmer*, which made several runs to the West Indies.

David moved to Upper Canada in 1801, settling in the new Quaker community in the north part of York County. With their two sons, John David and Israel, David and Phebe Willson walked up Yonge Street – then little more than a blazed trail – to claim their land grant on lot 10, in the second concession of East Gwillimbury. This land later formed the core of the village of Hope (Sharon).

In 1805 Willson "gained admittance according to my choice into the society of people called Quakers, after many years of tribulation and a rising and a falling of the mind; I served them according to their laws and discipline for seven years in all good faith and open communion."

During the War of 1812, the fundamentally pacifist Quaker settlers, living close to the military route that Yonge Street had become, suffered frequent persecution from the authorities. At the same time, David Willson's preaching led to his disownment from the Yonge Street Monthly Meeting, and along with several supporting families, he formed the Children of Peace.

Willson's group carried forward their core Quaker values of equality, charity, peace and education – beliefs alien to the colonial authorities and the British Crown – and "ornamented them with all the glory of Israel." He preached that he would take the

Quaker Testimony against War and "raise it higher as an Ensign to the Nations."

He likened his small group to the Old-Testament Israelites, lost in the wilderness, fleeing a cruel and despotic Pharaoh. He called on his rapidly growing congregation to build the "new Jerusalem" prophesied in the book of Revelation. At the centre of their community, they determined to build a Temple, "somewhat after the manner of Solomon."

Much of Willson's belief and behaviour cannot be understood except in reaction to the government-supported "hireling clergy" of the colonial Church of England. Willson's refusal to accept a salary as a minister stood out against the Anglican control of the funds from the Clergy Reserves, the special grant of one seventh of all land in the province rented out for the support of the "official" Church. He dressed in rags in imitation of Christ, and in contrast to the expected demeanour of an ordained minister of God's word. His pride in his lack of formal schooling – "my education was bounded by one year, and a considerable part of that time almost in my infancy" – was in sharp contrast to the university education of the Anglican clergy.

Willson was a homespun preacher: a man of the people and defender of their interests against the tightly knit establishment of merchants, official clergy and government. This "Family Compact" in turn accused him of losing "sight of affairs of a spiritual nature and expiating upon those of a worldly sort." Nonetheless, many of the new settlers in the province, immigrants from the south infused with republican idealism, found in Willson a palatable, if somewhat eccentric, alternative to the aristocratic pretensions of the British Colonial administration and the closely associated Church of England.

David Willson served as leader of the Children of Peace until his death on January 19, 1866.

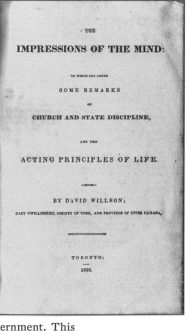

THE

IMPRESSIONS OF THE MIND:

TO WHICH ARE ADDED

SOME REMARKS

OF

CHURCH AND STATE DISCIPLINE,

AND THE

ACTING PRINCIPLES OF LIFE.

BY DAVID WILLSON;

EAST GWILLIMBURY, COUNTY OF YORK, AND PROVINCE OF UPPER CANADA,

TORONTO:
1835.

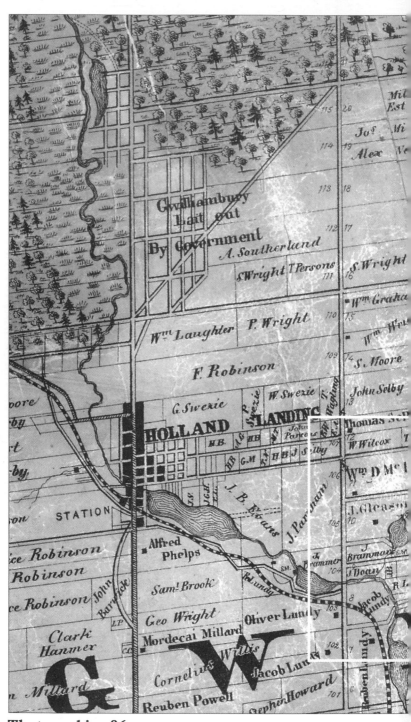

The township, 1860

(*Detail from the Tremain Map of York County*)

QUEENSVILLE

C Beary
P Wardle
Wm Hill
J Aylmar
C Wix
Jas. Milne
Ira Doan
Ed. Morton
Wm Willson
W Graham

J Doan
H. D. Stiles
Traviss Est
A. Nelson
John Aurbuthnot
John Aurbuthnot
John Reid

P Degeer
Wm Long
M. Curry
W Evans
O. Williams
C Foster

Sam! Trav
Sam! Trav
Isa
Sam
R.
Wn
W. Evans

J Graham
Robt Weddle
Wm Selby

Wm. Willson
G. Brammar
A. Doan
E. Doan
D. Doan
T. Wayling
A. Doan
Wm Reid
E. Doan

R. Weddle
T. Wayling

O. Williams
J. H. Willson
J. H. Willson
J. Lepard
B Williams

Charles Sta
J. Lepard
J. Willson

SHARON

J. Doan
J.D. Willson
P Rowen
Doan
Doan
Doan
Chas Haynes
Wm Kiteley
Isreal Wilson

C.D.W.R.J.W.
D. Willson
J. Lundy
John Doan
Jesse Doan
W. Knight
B. Lepard
J. Lundy
J. Maguire
John Terry
J. Collins
C Weddle

Job Hughs
E. Brammar
A. Rogers
A. Rogers
B Lepard
B Lepard
J. Curry
John Evans
E Hunter

W Purdy

W. Puro
J.C. Hucabo
Grave Yard
John Evan

The larger box corresponds to the aerial photograph of the modern locale, pages 16–17; the smaller box corresponds to the site view, pages 20–21.

The locale, today
(Based on the aerial view of 2002)

north ⋯⋯▸

1 Sharon Temple National Historic Site
2 Location of first meeting house (demolished) *Please note that this is private property.*
3 Children of Peace Burial Ground

Around the site

What follows here is a conventional sequence, but apart from the necessary presence of personal guides in the important interiors, visitors are encouraged to wander and appreciate the site on their own. Your own visit may well be different from this one.

Enter the site from the northeast, passing through what is now called the "gatehouse" and shop. This is a small structure built two concessions (about 3 km) to the north in the 1870s, first occupied as a village bread shop, then adapted as a bank branch, and ultimately made over as the Queensville public library, before being moved here in 1977. Viewed from the gatehouse, the Temple sits atop a gentle rise, framed by mature trees. In its active period, the complex of structures of the Children of Peace sat along the street frontage of David Willson's farm. Throughout most of the 19th century, the Temple also comprised a formidable formal fence that echoed the foursquare floor plan, surrounded in turn by a perimeter of mowed lawn.

The normal entry to the interior of the Temple is through the east door (facing the street), but the proper way to appreciate the building in its surroundings is to first walk all the way around it. The Children of Peace normally approached and circumnavigated the temple before entering.

Your guide will point out the salient features of the interior – you can hardly avoid Jacob's ladder which springs from the floor immediately at the east doorway – but the design and character of the interior are sketched out elsewhere in this guidebook.

Toward the street in front of the Temple is David Willson's study, originally in front of his residence to the south and next to – and formally very similar to – the now-vanished second meeting house. While its diminutive interior is not normally open to visitors, everything is clearly visible through windows on all four sides. Like the second meeting house, the study's portico provides shelter, a more social space than the rather more severe perimeter of the Temple. The contrast suggests that while it was integral to the complex, the Temple was clearly set apart from the rest in more ways than behind a fence.

Along the southern flank of the site is an informal row of structures. The white-painted clapboard shed is the cookhouse from the mid-1800s, which once adjoined the second meeting house for all the preparations for the feast days of the Children of Peace. Past an unpainted board-and-batten shed (the block house) is the board-and-batten museum building, built at the time of Canada's centennial in 1967 in the form of a 19th-century rural drive shed. The museum building houses a small interpretive display, with explanatory texts, images, video presentations and selected artifacts from the site's collections. Other parts of the museum's collections are stored in the building and may be available for study purposes (though many of the most delicate and valued artifacts and documents are in safekeeping away from the site).

The westernmost building in the row is a log cabin, generally typical of the earliest residences in the vicinity, and associated with the site as part of the former property of Jesse Doan, one of the family of builders chiefly responsible for the principal constructions of the Children of Peace. Follow the meandering grass path westward into the bush and trees around the back of the lot.

The pathway opens out to the back lawn once again along the north flank of the site and another row of historic structures. Three buildings – a granary and a drive shed, together with the painted clapboard house beyond – belonged to the master builder of the Temple's major buildings, Ebenezer Doan. The house, built in 1819, was rescued and moved to the site in 1958; the drive shed of 1818 and the granary of the 1830s were similarly rescued from their site in 1996. There is a fourth and rather more curious building: behind the Doan house is the round privy originally behind David Willson's own house, shaped so that (according to tradition) "the Devil could not catch you in a corner with your drawers down." As well, it may well be the oldest surviving outhouse in the province. Alongside the Doan house is an ongoing and ever-changing project: the annual recreation of a 19th-century household garden as the Doans might have had.

Once again, you stand in front of – or is it beside, or behind? – the Temple. The two official government plaques have been placed close to the street frontage to inform passersby of the provincial and national significance of the place. The remaining building of the complex, the Temperance Hall, lies across the pavement outside the site proper. For several decades part of the old East Gwillimbury township offices, the Hall is now a reception and gathering place for events at the site, as well as the 21st-century proxy for the 19th-century cookhouse.

The open space that makes up most of the western part of the site — once part of David Willson's croplands — was used as a municipal park and baseball ground for most of the early and middle parts of the 20th century. In the 1990s the western portion of the space was allowed to regenerate as a kind of wild grassland, planted with new saplings. You can wander through the parkland on a mowed path that offers picturesque distant views of the Temple in the 19th-century mode, though you will see in period photographs that the real 19th-century landscape was far less romantic.

The site, today
(Based on the aerial view of 2002)

1 Ebenezer Doan's house and garden
2 Doan farm buildings
3 David Willson's round outhouse
4 Temple

5 Gatehouse
6 Sharon Temperance Hall
7 David Willson's study
8 Museum row

9 Location of second meeting house
(demolished), and original site of study.
*Please note that this is private property,
and not part of the historic site.*

**David
Willson's study**

Moving buildings away from their original locations is severely discouraged under modern principles of historic preservation, even when structures can be rescued only by moving them away from an unavoidable threat. Nevertheless, buildings do get relocated; in the 19th century this was even a frequent occurrence. Only the Temple remains precisely where it was built. By circumstance, several structures have been relocated from other sites, and, of these, David Willson's study has had to be moved twice, first in 1918 to rescue it from destruction and then again in 1961 to rescue it from rot.

Despite its relocations, the study's interior and exterior reflect its state in the later years of Willson's life. It was completed in September 1829 and celebrated by "speeches and singing" at a public opening. With its colonnade and arches it can be seen both as part of the Temple "turned inside out," and as a model for the much larger second meeting house built after 1834. The study's roof lanterns and brick chimney are 20th-century approximations of missing originals, awaiting a more authentic reconstitution.

Until its 1918 rescue, the study sat almost on the street, near the northeastern corner of the second meeting house, not at all like the remote garden shelters or retreats of certain well-known writers. While an observer of 1861 noted that "inside is a good organ, a bed on which no one ever slept, a table, chairs, books, &c., and here Mr. Willson writes and studies, quite secluded from the outer world," the study's conspicuous position in front of the other Children of Peace buildings and Willson's own house suggests that Willson was quite pleased to watch the comings and goings of his community while he toiled for their spiritual benefit.

The first meeting house looked very much like an archetype for the Temple itself, as well as its Altar. Built in 1819 in the middle of the east frontage of Willson's farm, it followed the Quaker meeting-house type of roughly square plan, but with a precise forty feet to each side and a height of sixteen feet with generous glazing quite untypical for the period and the region. With one of Coates's organs installed in 1820, the building subsequently acquired its more popular name, the Music Hall. It was sold off for its lumber by David Willson's grandson Absalom in 1893.

The meeting houses

The second meeting house, three times the size of the first, was based on the form of David Willson's study, which had been completed in September 1829. On October 28, Willson wrote out a "bill of timber for the house of the Lord, Jacob's God and Israel's name," another of his poetic design specifications. ————→

Construction began in 1834, and like the Temple, its formal completion was stretched out until 1842. Its symmetry was bilateral rather than foursquare, and each pair of elevations was matched back to front, with the formal peculiarity of being wide and shallow in contrast to the conventional long and deep basilica form of "western" churches. Nevertheless, the precedent for the large shallow gable is not very hard to find in some of the same sources as those for Ezekiel's Temple, though the same caution about interpretation arises here as well—we do

Two lengthy sills of royal Oak
That we must soon prepare
It is my sense Jehovah spoke
Should be nine inches square
From End to End full Eighty four
With adding number one
Two added on to half a score
Across the sills to run
Five added on to three times ten
Or fifteen to a score
We have the full dimensions then
For Columns and for floor
In equal parts we'll then divide
To the small number three
Eleven feet eight from the outside
The Columns feet shall be ...
And when we do this bill complete
The lord will give us more
This is the boddy of the frame
Thats built in squares below
The tops misterious and plain
The measures none doth know.

↓

not know what David Willson knew, at least not yet.

The lumber of the second meeting house was offered for sale in 1912. (Absalom Willson had been keeping the Temple itself going as a tourist attraction by charging admission fees and, it seems, by selling off the other buildings.)

**The place
in time**

A single visit to the building cannot do it justice,
though frequent visits might overwhelm. Recall that
the Children of Peace came here just a few times a
year, and for meetings that were mostly quiet medita-
tions or the words of a single voice at a time. To occupy
the place for more than a few moments is to study it,
and that seems to be what Willson wanted. Different
seasons and changing qualities of light have profound
effects on what is at first glance a very simple space,
albeit "cluttered" in the centre with the Altar and an
array of poles that interfere with views of your neighbours across the way, or of performers or speakers no
matter where you sit or they stand. But if you have the
opportunity to sit in the Temple for a bit more time
and at different times, you might begin to sense what
the Children of Peace would have sensed when the
first or last spears of sunlight pierce right through the
building from one side to the other, or when storm or
snow or mist erase every shadow, or when the light
from candles inside the space matches the atmosphere
of dusk outside the building, and the central pillars
and arches and vaults dematerialize into a grove of
trees and the interior of a simple building transforms
into a precise and perfect harmony, an oasis of calm
at the centre of a restless world.

And that is why this really isn't a church for the
enactment of religious rituals. The only ritual, one that
requires no denomination, is to look and listen – and
marvel at the "chasteness of design unsurpassed."

The Temperance Hall

Samuel Hughes, a minister of the Children of Peace, was transformed by his experience in early 1832 into a firm temperance advocate. He conducted a systematic survey of the Townships of East Gwillimbury and Whitchurch, and found that there were "105 habitual drunkards out of a population of 1070 male adults." As he noted in his "Remarks on Intemperance," among these 105 habitual drunkards were "78 husbands who are parents of families, and from the best information, fathers of 312 children, and are companions, or rather abusers, of 78 afflicted women, who are bound to suffer under the government of madness and distraction." Hughes thereupon organized a Temperance Society among the members of the Children of Peace.

Temperance societies became increasingly common in Ontario in the late 1840s and early 1850s. The Children of Peace Temperance Society later became the Sharon Division, Sons of Temperance No. 222, and built a Temperance Hall in 1852. To house the township offices, the Hall was relocated next to the Sharon Temple grounds in 1913, a fitting symbol of the involvement of the Children of Peace in the Temperance movement from its inception in Ontario.

The Hall remained part of the township building up until the construction of the new municipal offices next door in the 1990s.

The Death of a Drunkard.

It was about the beginning of December 1831, that a poor man... left the village of Newmarket on a Friday evening to go to the Holland Landing; having with him a small sled, three jugs of whiskey and a little dog. Having drank too freely of the poison in the jugs, and a heavy snow storm beating in his face, he lost his road and wandered about in byeways until he was quite bewildered; and the cold increasing to an intense degree, together with the liquor he had drank rendered him stupid and unable to draw the sled. It appears he came sometime in the night to the neighbourhood of this village, and left his sled... He went a few rods into a field where, to appearance, he fell down, and not being able to rise, folded his arms about him and died. The little dog remained faithful to his master's goods at the sled till he was discovered by some of the neighbours, which led to the suspicion that the owner was lost, and search was immediately made for him. The snow however had fallen so deep that all efforts to discover the body proved fruitless... [the] awful truth, however, was ascertained about the middle of March, when the corpse was discovered frozen hard, lying directly under the pathway of sleighs where it had remained nearly four months...

When some preparations were made, we assembled to take up the body. After loosening the skeleton and turning it over, and I had removed the jug that still remained close by his side, the spectacle he presented produced in me feelings beyond description. And what was still more to be abhorred, the very man in whose service he died, & for whom the whiskey was bought, was at that moment reeling to and fro over the corpse in a state of intoxication. Who could look upon such a scene without sorrow of heart, or without resolving to give all his aid and influence to Temperance Societies? I fastened up the box into which the body was put: my mind was overcharged, my soul revolted at the scene, — I turned my back and went away.

Samuel Hughes, Hope, August 1832.

The timber-framed Doan house is remarkable for its survival, even though it no longer sits where it was built in 1819. It is not clear how many years the house remained occupied after Doan died in 1866, but it had fallen into (dis)use as a storage building before modern services of piped water and electricity arrived at the farm. And because it was spared the periodic modernization typical of most inhabited dwellings, its early 19th-century character survived on account of its long decades of neglect. Moved to the site of the Temple in 1958, it now displays not only a rare domestic space of a relatively prosperous early settler in the region, but also the dwelling of one of the principal families of the Children of Peace, and the man most responsible for their shared buildings.

Ebenezer Doan's house

To the learned eye (which in this case belongs to W. John McIntyre) the interior of the house brings to light a particular mix of British and German cultural legacy imported from Pennsylvania, further blended by circumstance in the new farmlands of Upper Canada. As late as the 1840s, most of the dwellings in upper York County were single-storey log constructions (like Jesse Doan's residence across the field), so that Ebenezer's two-storey house seems almost a mansion for the period. In their early decades the households of the Children of Peace were larger than those of other groups, so a relatively larger house should not have been surprising. But Ebenezer's is notable as well for its finishing and furnishing in an amalgam of styles still anchored far back in the 18th century. Most significant is the evident attention paid to the smallest details of joinery (in what they call these days "vernacular" architecture), signs of both understanding of visual effect and patience in execution.

For a long period after 1958 the exterior was painted white, as it had been during its disused decades, but professional paint archaeology revealed an original brick-red colour, whose restoration has proven difficult to match.

As part of the museum program of the Sharon Temple site, the Doan house is often used for interpretive programs, and its interior is usually open to be wandered into as part of any site visit.

The place in detail

At first, David Willson's own words on his design provides most of what the visitor needs to understand. But there are many, many small touches to seek out. Both the bigger spatial relationships and smaller finishing details are only crudely visible in photographs; a true impression cannot really be formed except on the spot. It is impossible to say which is more important — the design or the execution, the mind or the hand. The final results are indivisible that way.

Although the Temple was made to be equally accessible from all directions by design, the traditional "ceremonial" entrance has been through the east door, facing the street. As soon as you enter and immediately confront Jacob's Ladder, it is evident that this door might be more equal than the others. When the Children of Peace entered here, they passed around either side of the ladder to their seats. Only the musicians ascended the ladder, in order that their unseen voices and instruments would make "heavenly" sounds while the congregation listened and prepared to give proper attention, and alms, to their community.

The floor is slightly terraced in foursquare plan so that even those seated around the perimeter can see over the heads of those in "front", but since this is theatre-in-the-square, the views are invariably of other people, or of the sixteen pillars, or out the windows, or of the central Altar (what the York Pioneers tended instead to call the Ark, so both names are used). Apart from the benches around the perimeter walls, the traditional seating was on individual chairs, a few of which survive on display (together with a growing number of handcrafted reproductions made as part of efforts to raise maintenance funds for the Temple). There are two of Richard Coates's organs from the vanished meeting houses, two of the banners carried about by the Children of Peace in their processions and the occasional small display of items from the museum's collections, but the interior is no longer the artifact gallery it was through most of the 20th century. The Temple is generally kept as unoccupied as possible, available on the one hand for special events and performances and on the other hand for quiet visits and contemplation.

Unless you are fortunate enough to hear a musical performance — on occasion an organist may play a tune on one of the organs — you may wonder about the reputed acoustic properties of the Temple, since its interior doesn't sound so marvellous with a chatter of voices, and it is sometimes even hard to hear. The foursquare plan is not so egalitarian for sound, nor so tolerant of certain kinds of instruments. But when properly arranged with the right configuration of instruments and voices, the building is in fact exceptionally and famously musical.

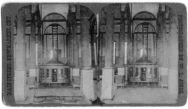

(See page 44.)

Quaker words, Quaker music

Among Protestant denominations, the Quakers are distinct for their rejection of music in worship. Congregational singing was an empty form, they argued: "the Almighty was not to be worshipped by the workmanship of man's hands." Worship must focus upon the word of God as revealed by the "Inner Light," the spirit of God within the soul. Believing fundamentally that the spirit of God was equally available to all, they endorsed the protestant credo of the "ministry of all believers." They also took seriously the biblical injunction: "Take no thought beforehand what ye shall speak, neither do ye premeditate: but whatsoever shall be given you in that hour that speak ye: for it is not ye that speak but the Holy Ghost" (Mark 13:11). Thus, "ministry" was spontaneous, directed only by the leadings of the spirit, which could call any member, man or woman, to preach. Until the moment that someone felt that call to stand and deliver a message, members sat, waiting in silence.

The Children of Peace proceeded in grand procession last Sunday afternoon, with music and banners, from the foot of Yonge Street, along King Street to the York Hotel, at which place their principal speaker, Mr Willson delivered to a very large and attentive assemblage of the townspeople an energetic discourse upon the vices and follies of the age we live in.

The band of music was very full, and the performers deserve the highest commendations. The hymns were original in their composition, and the voices of the singers exceedingly sweet and harmonious. Such a concert of sacred music as the Children of Peace gave last Sunday in York would do honour, in the execution, to any part of christendom.

Colonial Advocate, September 26, 1833

David Willson, in contrast, began to "sing in the ministry" as early as 1811. He regarded music as another facet of ministry, a spontaneous expression of the Inner Light. Willson came to boast, "I never repeat one communication twice over, nor sing one old hymn in worship: bread from heaven is our lot — descending mercies." The constant production of music, like manna from heaven, was a sign of its sacred origin. Willson wrote new words to a fixed set of melodies for each service; "They compose all their own hymns and psalms to suit the occasion on which they were sung." These hymns, eventually numbering in the thousands, were then kept in the Ark for posterity, in a special "Book of Sacred Record."

At the beginning and end of each worship service, Willson would "read out" a hymn, line by line, which would then be sung back by a choir, and then the congregation. The lining-out of hymns had been the traditional singing style of the 18th century, when hymn books were expensive and rare. Songs were sung *a cappella*, resulting in slow, improvised singing in which each singer was allowed to decorate the tunes as he or she saw fit.

Music was also performed by the band organized by Coates, and by a choir of "virgins" (schoolgirls). The musical accompaniment provided by the choir, band and organs was in large part responsible for the fame — or infamy — which accrued to the Children of Peace.

In 1846, the Children of Peace hired Daniel Cory, a music teacher from Boston, to give them "systematic training in all the rudiments of singing." It was Cory who taught them the unison singing of the Protestant mainstream, and for that purpose, the sect published the first of his hymn books in 1846, *Hymns and Prayers for the Children of Sharon: To be sung in Worship on Sabbath Days*. Willson published two more hymn books before his death.

The leader of the Children of Peace had pondered the concept of the Temple for a long time before he and the congregation began to build. In 1822, Willson composed a poem entitled "The Lord's Celebration" (later printed as a broadside), which proclaimed his architectural plan – and schedule – for constructing the Temple.

David Willson's personal illumination

Apart from the number of windows – suggesting the Temple of his vision started off more like a two-storey version of the Temple's first floor, perhaps an enlargement of the recently completed first meeting house – these verses comprise the only surviving documentation of the architectural design he intended.

In peace I write this structure The Lord to gratify,
And raise to him an altar built for his name alone,
That when he comes descending he'll make with me his home.

In Eighteen Hundred Twenty with five this date I'll pen,
We'll fasten the four corners and lay the bottom stone;
United with my Brothers we'll build this house alone.

Hewn stone is the foundation well beaten into square,
And then we'll raise the pillars aloft the work shall go,
Plan'd by the Architecture that formed this globe below.

We'll ring it round with columns their number Twelve shall be,
To mind us of apostles that once the earth hath trod;
We'll try to follow after and build a throne to God.

In the midst of these columns we'll raise the royal square;
We'll never bow to Masons nor ask them of their art;
The skillfull Architecture is Grace within the heart.

We'll raise our semicircles and spring our arches high;
He is the executor that gives to me the plan,
He'll show the art to Woman that's bone of bone to man.

We'll chain the globe by quarters it on the top shall hang,
Like gold it shall be gilded and union testify,
High hanging by four spires to please the seeing eye.

Its length shall be feet sixty its breadth be equal square,
To North and South be facing to East and West the same;
The union of best timber shall build this royal frame.

We'll clothe it with white colours with green spread on the brow,
Its height to plates be twenty with adding number one
In twenty-five begin it in thirty-two get done.

An altar to all nations a standing pillar here,
With forty-eight bright windows no darkness there shall hide
With bars and gates surrounded to keep it clean inside.

On Ararat we'll place it and Peace its name shall be,
A house of lasting blessings where grace is multiplied,
A rest for every nature and God is the inside.

Its ornaments and gilding no architect can tell,
Its weights are without number its scales were never known,
And endless is its measures like mercies of the Throne.

Explaining it to Emily McArthur decades later, probably in his eighties, he might have become less lyrical, but no less clear, that his most expressive construction was, from his first vision to his last, most especially and deliberately symbolic.

The puzzle of the Temple's origins

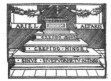

The Temple of the Children of Peace is the realization of a tradition of a vision of the divine. Yet, though never shy about speaking and recording his beliefs, David Willson left behind no clear description in words or diagrams of the Temple itself and the inspirations for its design. On one hand, this "mystery" is hardly mysterious, since such plans and drawings were exceedingly rare in any case for the period, and even less likely to have survived. On the other hand, such documents normally exist primarily to confirm some contract of understanding between client and builder. For the Temple – and all the buildings of the Children of Peace – client and builder were the same people.

It is evident from the building itself and from historical accounts that the master builder was Ebenezer Doan, assisted by his cabinetmaker brother John and other Doans, together with David Willson himself and his own relations, all presumably aided by anyone else in the Children of Peace who could wield hammer or saw. To be a member of the Children of Peace was to be, by subscription and participation, and whether male or female, a builder of the meeting houses, and especially the Temple.

Cabinetmakers and carpenters of the period worked by memory and example, learning from previous pieces and buildings as well as from printed manuals and illustrations, though these were all in limited supply in the pioneer regions. To manage the construction of an unprecedented form would need both considerable skill in execution and a shared understanding of what the construction was supposed to look like at the end. Everyone knew what a barn should look like before construction started but what would Willson's Temple look like? The questions of where his vision came from and how he got that vision across to his fellow builders continue to stimulate curiosity.

Local tradition and academic research have attributed the design of the Sharon Temple to a specific vision that David Willson had of the Temple of Solomon in Jerusalem (that is, the First Temple of the Kingdom of Israel), based in turn on certain of the descriptions in the biblical books of I Kings, II Chronicles, Ezekiel and Revelation. For his part, Willson seems to have been careful not to proclaim that his Temple was intended to replicate Solomon's, but his longstanding fascination with the biblical Israelites and his writings about reconciling Christianity with those ancient traditions is quite clear in his sermons and writings.

Those biblical texts about the first Temple do not agree among themselves very well, nor does Willson's written specification for his own Temple match any of

them. Except, in some respects, for Ezekiel's—which was itself a vision of what the first Temple should have been rather than claiming to be a description of what it had been. And that should have been far

more interesting theologically and spiritually to a temperament like David Willson's.

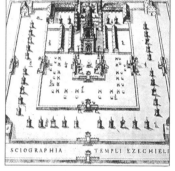

SCIOGRAPHIA   TEMPLI EZECHIELI

The Altar of Burnt-Offering according to the Learned DEAN PRIDEAUX.

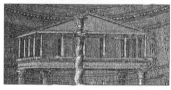

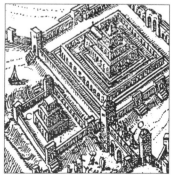

From Solomon to David, in pictures

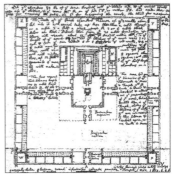

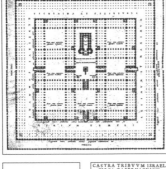

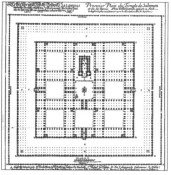

UNIVERSI TEMPLI HIEROSOLYMITANI ORTHOGRAPHIA QVAE OSTENDIT ORIENTALEM FACIEM MVRI ATRII EXTERIORIS ET PARTEM MVRI PORTICVS GENTIVM QVAE DEINDE DICTA EST SALOMONIS

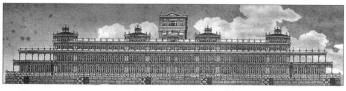

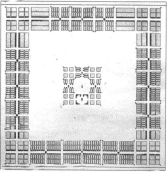

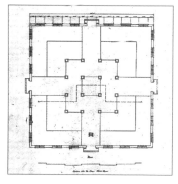

From Solomon to David, in words

The model has survived more than three centuries and is on permanent public display at the Museum of Hamburg History.

According to the Old Testament Bible, the Temple of Solomon was built perhaps 3,000 years ago, and destroyed without a trace perhaps 2,700 years ago. Afterwards, in exile in Babylon, the prophet Ezekiel, a former temple priest, envisioned the restoration of the "ancient tribes" of Israel and the restoration of their Temple in a new Jerusalem – and he described, in a mix of reminiscences and prophecies, his idealized Temple in the book that bears his name. Though a second Temple did get built, and was itself almost completely destroyed, the "original" and its divine inspiration were discussed, argued, fantasized, imagined, sketched out and prayed for, by Jews and Christians alike, for 2,000 more years. Fragments of that divine design appeared (and still do) in sacred architecture in both Christian and Islamic realms.

In 1600, an architecturally trained Spanish Jesuit, Juan Bautista Villalpando, "calculated" and published in Rome a volume of Ezekiel's visions in Baroque, counter-Reformation style. The book was disseminated widely: copies and emulations of his plans and elevations appeared in print frequently over the next two centuries and more. Gerhard Schott of Hamburg commissioned a wooden model at 1:500 scale in 1694, which travelled through Europe. Its public display in London in 1724 caught the notice of Sir Isaac Newton, who reinterpreted it and published his own reconstruction of Ezekiel's vision of the first Temple in Cambridge in 1728, followed by John Wood's version in Bath in 1741.

Solomon's Temple and its associated myths, long held as staples of Freemasonry and the carpenter's trade, re-emerged throughout the 18th century as key features in western popular culture, revived not just in those academic texts but also in printed Bibles and in inspirational sermons – such as one delivered and published by one Reverend John Stanford to a meeting of carpenters in New York City in 1792, at a time when a young David Willson was apprenticing in New York with his brother. As Willson matured, married and entered the Quaker faith, he adopted the inspiration of the archetypal builder that goes back to Solomon, and preached to incorporate that spirit into an authentic Christian life and worship. All the while, Villalpando's rendering of Ezekiel's version of Solomon's Temple continued to reappear, in picture form, in the pages of popular editions of the Bible published in Britain and America in the early 1800s.

There are evident correspondences between the plans of Villalpando's reconstruction of Ezekiel's vision and Willson's ground plan, and between the tiered elevations of parts of Villalpando with the Sharon elevations. There are also resemblances between other Villalpando elevations and Willson's second meeting house and his study. Perhaps one or another family in the Children of Peace had one of the bibles where Ezekiel's vision is pictured, or perhaps Willson came across one or another of the 18th-century recapitulations of Ezekiel in his time in New York. Least likely is that David Willson invented all those symbolic strategies and forms without invoking the traditions that preceded him.

The Temple at Sharon – both a building and a landscape – appears very much like a model of the entirety of Ezekiel's vision as diagrammed by Villalpando, and at the same time a reconstruction of a small, human-scaled corner of that vision, in which is nested John Doan's Altar, a smaller model within the larger one.

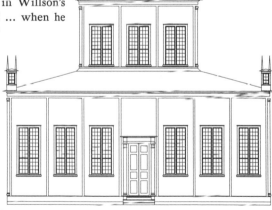

And at the same time, the Temple as a whole, with its tiered form, is an altar at a colossal scale, meant to receive, in Willson's words, "The Lord ... when he comes descending."

Both Ezekiel's vision and David Willson's Temple comprise a sacred and deliberate geometry of squares within squares, with central entrances on every side, defining a set of precincts more and more sacred as one approaches the innermost – and, quite deliberately, the innermost cannot be entered at all.

The tradition of rethinking and reconstructing Solomon's Temple is a very long one. Willson's vision of the most apt form of an earthly accommodation for the divine had to be based on that long accumulation of concepts and images just as much as his impromptu dreams and visions. Otherwise his congregation would not have been able to understand and build it.

The timber framework

The Temple is mostly wood, from the towering twelve- and fourteen-inch timbers comprising the "royal square" of Faith, Hope Love and Charity, down to slim strips of lath, half-inch-wide decorative wooden reeds and quarter-inch slivers of panelling. The structural frame is more or less that of a heavy timber barn, though for it to be at all comprehensible, the diagram of its skeleton leaves out the smaller floor, wall and window framing that are big enough by themselves to hold up a barn, too.

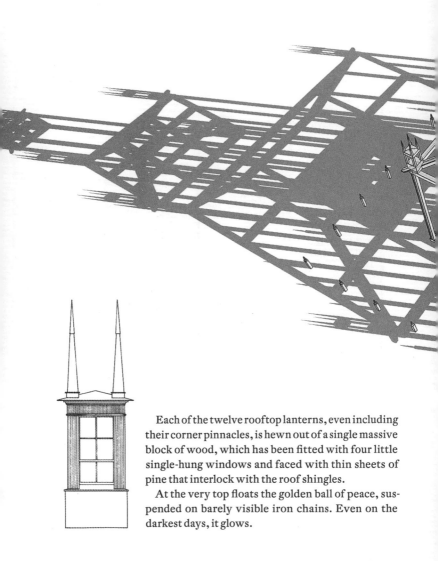

Each of the twelve rooftop lanterns, even including their corner pinnacles, is hewn out of a single massive block of wood, which has been fitted with four little single-hung windows and faced with thin sheets of pine that interlock with the roof shingles.

At the very top floats the golden ball of peace, suspended on barely visible iron chains. Even on the darkest days, it glows.

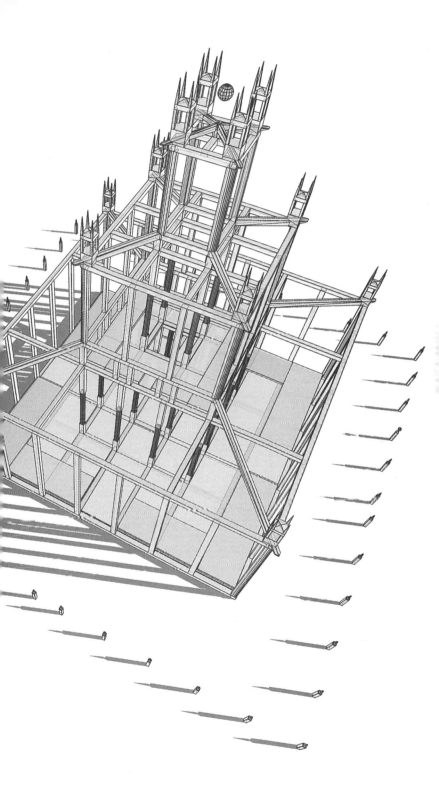

Richard Coates

Many of the Quakers who joined the Children of Peace were skilled craftsmen, but the Quaker "testimony" on plainness discouraged them from embracing the arts; adornment of any kind was considered little but a sign of pride. Thus, when David Willson's vision commanded him to "ornament the Church with all the glory of Israel," the sect had to turn to an outsider, Richard Coates, for guidance. Coates, a former British Army Bandmaster, exerted tremendous influence on the art and music by which the Children of Peace came to be known outside their community. He built their organs, formed and initially led their band, painted "the symbolic decorations of the interior of the Temple at Sharon," and painted the banners that they carried in front of their processions.

Coates was reputed to have played in a British Army band during the Peninsular War, and to have been a bandmaster at the Battle of Waterloo. Like many officers decommissioned after the Napoleonic wars, he immigrated to Upper Canada, settling in York (Toronto) in 1818. Coates had a large house on Duke Street in York, unusual for the organ of "some pretensions" he had built inside (now on display in the Temple), as well as "an elegantly finished little pleasure yacht of about nine tons' burden" constructed in the yard. He also made a four-foot telescope, now in the Temple's museum collection. Shortly after his arrival in York, he was commissioned by the Children of Peace to build the first of their organs – said, in fact, to be the first built in Ontario. It was at this time that he also gave lessons to the Children of Peace in the rudiments of musical performance, teaching members how to play the instruments of a brass band.

The details of Coates's life are sketchy. He was born November 30, 1778, in Thornton Dale, Yorkshire, England, and married Isabella Smith on November 5, 1805. Isabella was the niece of Sir Joshua Reynolds, president of the Royal Academy and an eminent portrait painter. But nothing is known of Coates's education or where he refined his musical or artistic skills.

In 1831 Coates moved to Trafalgar Township east of Oakville where he acquired land and established a water-powered sawmill and threshing mill. He died at age 89, on January 29, 1868, in Rodney, Aldborough Township, Ontario.

When Richard Coates petitioned for land in 1824, he described himself as a painter (both house and portrait). Material evidence of his skills survives: two of the four banners he painted for the Children of Peace now hang in the Sharon Temple. He is as well the probable artist of the only known portrait of David Willson.

In 1819 the Children of Peace completed their first meeting house (later known as the Music Hall) on part of Willson's farm fronting Leslie Street. Inside, as described by William Lyon Mackenzie,

> the first object which catches the eye is the organ. In the centre of the house a platform is raised about five feet high and is support[ed] by four simple columns. It is surrounded by a railing below, and inside of this there are seats apparently designed for the musicians. The upper part of the platform also is surrounded with a rail – and on this rostrum the organ stands. It reaches nearly to the arched roof of the house.

Organs

The barrel organ on its podium (both now in the Temple) became the physical centre of the meeting house, the first thing seen no matter which door was entered, and so a fitting symbol of the new importance of music in their meetings for worship.

Coates's organ for Sharon was unusual, much larger than most barrel organs of the period. Its apparent size would have seemed all the larger as it perched on its raised platform in the first meeting house. The organ itself is 8½ feet high, 4½ feet wide and 2½ feet deep. It is fully chromatic, with more than a hundred wooden pipes in four ranks (one 8-inch, two 4-inch, and a 2-inch), a compass of 37 notes, and 133 wooden flue pipes (one 4-inch rank is incomplete). Despite its size, it can be operated by a single player, cranking the barrel with the left hand, pumping the bellows with the left foot, operating the stops with the right hand, while balancing on the right foot.

When David Willson decided to introduce music into the worship services of the Children of Peace, he was faced with a very down-to-earth problem: teaching people who had no musical skills to play. One of the sect's initial responses to this problem, in 1820, was to commission a barrel organ from Richard Coates to provide musical accompaniment. Barrel organs had become popular in England in late 18th and early 19th centuries to meet the needs of small parish churches that lacked an organist. Prior to that time, a variety of other humble instruments filled in for the larger organs of city churches.

The largest of the organs built by Coates was a keyboard organ (now in the Temple) completed in 1848 for the second meeting house. The organ stood against the back wall of the second meeting house between the two rear doors. It stands about fourteen feet high, housed in an impressive case assembled in three towers; to the front are three semi-circles of gilded dummy pipes which hide the wooden pipework within. The organ has a manual 49-note direct mechanical keyboard, four drawstops, and 200 wooden flue pipes in four ranks. A manual bellows is pumped from the left side.

In the seventh year, they made an Altar

(*Detail from an undated stereo card in the collection of Steven Evans*)

This pair of photographs can be viewed in three dimensions, with or without a stereoscope.

Richard Coates seems to have been Toronto's first resident artist. To all appearances self-taught, notwithstanding his wife's relation to the eminent Sir Joshua Reynolds, Richard Coates painted two sophisticated symbolic banners for the Children of Peace. Flags and banners had a long history as iconic emblems of group identity in the marches and processions of churches, fraternal organizations, political movements and craft associations. The images on Coates's banners made visible the shared vision that led Willson and the Children of Peace to reconstruct Solomon's Temple.

The banners captured these associations with the artistic symbols of their times. The first, "Peace," came from Willson's vision of June 21, 1812. A long-haired woman identified as the "Church of

Christ" is robed in red, "the blood of the Christian martyrs" and bears two children, "the two dispensations," Jewish law and Christianity. Here, the "true church" combines both dispensations, like the Children of Peace in their Temple.

The second banner, "Plenty," also shows two children: the naked child on the right, Moses, points to an open book, the revelation of scripture and the law. The child on the left, Christ, holds a sealed book representing his direct revelation from God. He points to a descending dove, representing the Holy Spirit, available equally to all.

For a small, rural group which never had more than 350 members, the musical accomplishments of the Children of Peace were remarkable. It was said that "Popular music was whistled in Sharon a year before first heard in Old Toronto." Yet only one member of the group made an actual living from music: John Doan Graham.

Graham was born on January 11, 1846, the last of five children of William Graham and Elizabeth Doan. John D. Graham replaced his uncle, Jesse Doan, as leader of the band in 1866. Although little is known of his life outside of his musical career, one friend noted that he was an ardent admirer of Mark Twain: "He sounded like Mark Twain, he looked like him almost to the point of being his double, he dressed like him and even named his son, Mark Twain Graham."

Under Graham's leadership, the band became semi-professional. They purchased silver instruments in the United States for about $1,500, and donned blue uniforms. With their new instruments, they became known as the Sharon Silver Band. They would play in nearby towns, as well as on the pleasure cruises then plying Lake Simcoe during the summer months. The band was good enough to enter a competition at the Philadelphia Centennial Exposition of 1876, and to win a cash prize.

Graham made frequent fall trips to New York and Boston to learn the latest music. He purchased a "single selection, and each bandsman's part was copied by their leader into books of blank forms... Overtures, serenades, and selections from standard operas are among their repertoire."

However, Graham was not satisfied to merely play the works of others; he was also a composer in his own right. At least three published works are known: *Canada's Jubilee Greeting to her Gracious Majesty Queen Victoria* (1897), *The Flag of Canada* (1899) and the *Doan Centennial Hymn* (1908).

John Doan Graham and the Silver Band

Although like most other residents of Sharon, Graham initially earned his living in agriculture, by the time of his marriage he chose to work as a musician, music teacher and piano tuner. Such became his teaching and leadership skills that the band could "transpose the music as they played, thereby saving the trouble of rewriting the original score in a different key."

The nationalistic fervour of John D. Graham's work was typical of most other sheet music published in Canada at the time. *The Flag of Canada*, for example, begins:

The Flag of our Dominion is the Union Jack so dear,
Upon its folds the Maple Leaf
and Beaver shine so clear.
It safely guards our peaceful homes
and proudly rides the sea.
Where ere our Sons or Daughters
roam beneath that flag they're free.

Paupers, politics and charity

The Temple was never intended to be a "church." It was used just once a month to collect alms for the poor. The charity collected in the Temple was part of a larger design to help preserve the independence and livelihoods of local farmers and artisans. The alms enabled construction of the first shelter for the homeless in the province. In 1832, the Children of Peace used some of these funds to create a credit union, from which those in need could borrow small sums. The group instituted a form of land-sharing, so that young families could "borrow" land, just as they could money, until such time as they could afford to pay. And the Children of Peace helped establish the "Farmer's Storehouse Company," the first producers' co-operative in Canada. The Farmer's Storehouse was built on Toronto's waterfront, next to the market square. Members of the co-operative could store wheat there for transport to Montreal and buy their shop goods. In this way, members avoided falling in debt to Toronto's mercantile elite.

In Upper Canada a man could be jailed indefinitely for a debt as small as £2, and the initial debt was often inflated by legal costs. The merchants to whom the debts were owed and the lawyers who collected these fees were frequently those who acquired the debtor's land at cut prices at the Sheriff's sale. This had, apparently, been the fate of David Willson's stepbrother, robbed of his land and mill by the Solicitor General. Some of these same lawyers, part of the tightly knit Family Compact, had broken into William Lyon Mackenzie's print shop in 1826 and destroyed his press for having pointed to this abuse. The Family Compact controlled the non-elected Legislative Council, which routinely rejected every attempt for democratic reforms.

Willson began to preach up and down the length of Yonge Street and in Toronto during the 1830s, drawing large crowds with music, processions and a message which addressed "the question of taxes, tribute money, and the appropriation of revenue, with a good effect, and proved the intimacy of the relation which subsists between civil and religious rights." This popular mix of religion and politics reflected a broad public unease with Family Compact's attempts to entrench the Church of England in Upper Canada. Despite the fact most of the population belonged to other denominations, one seventh of all land in the province was deeded to the "official" church.

In 1828, William Lyon Mackenzie, newspaper editor, politician, first mayor of Toronto, travelled north of muddy York (Toronto) to the village of "Hope" for the first time, lured by the charismatic preaching of David Willson. Mackenzie found

> a village composed of about forty or fifty remarkably neat, clean dwellings; but what gives the most imposing effect is, the handsome newly built Temple, which is built nearly on the summit of the hill, and is now nearly finished. It is intended for their public worship, and is built somewhat after the manner of Solomon's Temple. The new church or chapel of the Children of Peace is certainly calculated to inspire the beholder with astonishment; its dimensions – its architecture – its situation – are all so extraordinary.

William Lyon Mackenzie

His fateful meeting with Willson sparked a collaboration that would, through political petitions, demonstrations and active rebellion, bring about their shared vision of a democratic Canada.

The political activity of the Children of Peace increased with time, as their involvement with Mackenzie grew. He supported their petitions for the incorporation of the Farmer's Storehouse, which would have allowed them to take the deed to their land. The bill was rejected twice by the Family Compact in the Legislative Council. Abuses such as this drove Mackenzie to organize a "Grand Convention of Delegates" to nominate democratic reform candidates, at which the Children of Peace figured prominently; it eventually led to the formation of the province's first political party, the democratic reform-minded Canadian Alliance Society. The first action of this party was to organize a province-wide petition to implement a "Provincial Loan Bank": the Farmer's Storehouse plan on a provincial basis. Though this scheme proved no more successful, these Reformers did finally manage to develop the "Bank of the People," to counter the "Bank of Upper Canada" controlled by the Family Compact.

The Reformers ultimately shaped a set of public institutions that emulated those of the Children of Peace, including the Bank of the People, the House of Industry (a shelter for the homeless, housed in the building which was once the headquarters of the Canadian Alliance Society), the Mechanics Institute, and the Home District Mutual Insurance Company. These institutions sought to provide economic protection to the "farmers and mechanics" – the working, or "operative" classes – in the tumultuous years before the Rebellion of 1837.

Rebellion

William Lyon Mackenzie mobilized the prominent activist Reformers across the Home District (today's York Region) in the ill-fated rebellion of 1837. A widespread depression beginning in 1836 had aggravated the already desperate circumstances of many Canadian colonial farmers, pushing them to the brink of ruin. In the early part of 1837, the Governor General, Lord Russell, issued his "Ten Resolutions" in an attempt to quell agitation and bring a brewing rebellion in Lower Canada (Quebec) to heel. The draconian measures sparked widespread fear that the constitution would be abrogated and the elected

Legislative Assembly suspended in Upper Canada as well. In early December, at Mackenzie's urging, the farmers of the Home District took up arms in aid of a similar rebellion in Lower Canada.

Younger members of the Children of Peace, urged on by a local member of the Assembly, Samuel Lount, answered Mackenzie's call. These included Jesse Doan, son of John Doan (the cabinetmaker who constructed the Ark standing at the centre of the Temple), Jesse's brother Charles, a shopkeeper, and John David Willson (David Willson's son). About twenty others from the village marched on Toronto in December 1837.

Mackenzie, however, was no military leader, and the poorly organized and poorly armed band of rebels who had collected north of the city at Montgomery's Tavern was scattered after a single melee. Two members of the Children of Peace died in the brief skirmish; James Henderson and James Kavanagh became the first of numerous martyrs this small group would offer in the defence of democracy. In the aftermath of the rebellion, the vindictive militia burned down Montgomery's Tavern, and "it was only with difficulty that the militia could be restrained from destroying the Temple." Many innocent members of the Children of Peace were arrested and jailed for months. Samuel Lount was hanged for treason.

With many others, Jesse and Charles Doan whiled away the hours in the overcrowded Toronto jail by carving "Rebellion Boxes" as mementoes for their loved ones. Mary, Charles's pregnant wife, wrote him, "I am well at present, and so is the little child. I think its name will be David Willson Doan, there is a great majority, and I think he will get a box." The baby was born twelve days later; Charles remained in jail for five months.

These modest mementoes served as powerful reminders of the ideals which led these men to take their stand against the powerful clique of merchants who ruled the province. Often inscribed with words like "Liberty" and "Independence," the boxes put a brave face on the uncertain future confronting both prisoners and their families.

The box carved by Jesse strikes a melancholy note of hope almost lost. Made after seven long months in jail, its sides bear the names of martyrs Samuel Lount and Peter Matthews. On the remaining sides are the following verses:

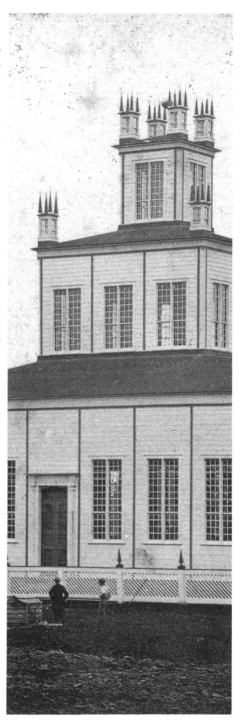

> Oft clinging to the massy grate,
> To catch a glimpse of heavens fair light.
> Uncertain as to future fate,
> Yet trust in God to set all right.

> Now summer is her robes of green
> Looks smiling fair and gay,
> Yet not a charm for those are seen,
> Whose rights are torn away.

Robert Baldwin and "Responsible Government"

Undaunted by the repressive political atmosphere after the failed rebellion, the Children of Peace joined with other reformers in 1839 to organize "Durham meetings" in support of Lord Durham's Report, which sought to alleviate the long-standing grievances that had sparked the rebellions in Upper and Lower Canada. Lord Durham recommended the adoption of "responsible government" and the union of the two Canadas. Responsible government entailed cabinet rule answerable to the elected assembly rather than to the British crown and its representative, the Governor General.

However, at the Durham Meeting for the Home District, set for Finch's tavern on Yonge Street on October 15, 1839, "the Mayor of the City, several Alderman, Magistrates, and other public functionaries," led a riot at which one young member of the Children of Peace, David Leppard, aged nineteen, was killed. His violent death at the hands of a Tory mob, with the complicity of Mayor and magistrates, provoked a parliamentary inquiry – there had been no arrests or investigations into the death, with the unmistakable implication that there was no protection against government-supported violence. The parliamentary inquiry affirmed the peaceful democratic rights of the "Durhamites" under the law.

The Reformers, now under the leadership of Robert Baldwin, pressed for the implementation of Durham's report, and especially for responsible government. Baldwin, a lawyer and constitutional expert, had stepped down from the Executive Council (cabinet) in 1836, when the Lieutenant Governor, Sir Francis Bond Head, had refused to accept the principle of cabinet responsibility to the elected Assembly. Bond Head's intransigence had set the stage for the Rebellion.

Baldwin had been elected in 1841 in Mackenzie's old seat, the Fourth Riding of York, which included the village of Hope, as well as in the riding of Hastings to the east. When the leader of the Lower-Canadian Reformers, Louis-Hippolyte LaFontaine, lost his bid for a seat in Terrebonne, Quebec, Baldwin offered him the opportunity to run in the Fourth Riding of York. With the support of the Children of Peace, the Fourth Riding could claim to have elected both the men who became known as the fathers of responsible government.

Both LaFontaine and Baldwin and were named to the Cabinet, where they pressed for the adoption of democratic reforms. But their 1843 bill to limit the Loyal Orange Order, responsible for much of the Tory-sponsored political violence, was held up by the new Governor General, Sir Charles Metcalfe. At Baldwin's instigation the Cabinet resigned as it had in 1836, sparking a further constitutional crisis. Metcalfe prorogued parliament for a full year, and democratic government in the colony became a farce. In 1843, a newly formed Reform Association organized meetings throughout the province. The meeting for the Fourth Riding of York coincided with the annual feast in honour of David Willson's birthday and drew more than 3000 people. This strong expression helped solidify public opinion against Metcalfe and contributed to the broad public consensus that the time for responsible government had come. After three years of struggle with Metcalfe, Baldwin and LaFontaine would finally win a landslide victory in both provinces in 1847 which cemented the principle of Responsible Government.

Jacob's Ladder and John's reeds

Jacob's Ladder rises almost vertically from the east entrance and segues into an attic staircase at the top. Its treads are astonishingly thin, and strong. The arc of its profile is a visual masterstroke, since a straight-line ladder would appear to sag even if it really didn't. This visual tactic is similar to the ancient practice of entasis (the bulging middle) of the columns.

And while the interior walls and ceilings are faced rather conventionally with thin coats of plaster and painted wooden panelling, there are many very subtle embellishments in the many strips of half-round "reeding," a detail of furniture far more than of architecture. Reeding is a feature of cabinetry built by John Doan and a few other makers in different parts of eastern North America in the late 18th and early 19th centuries.

The side panels of the ladder are clad with the same half-round reeding that appears throughout the interior, including strips bordering the ceiling coves and the miniaturized trim of the central Altar. Outside the Temple, the same reeding accents the lanterns at each corner of the three roofs, strips of soffit and cornice on all elevations, the outside panels of all four pairs of doors, and the building's corners on all levels.

Reeding was used as well in the demolished second meeting house, inside and out.

The exterior walls of the Temple are made with horizontal boards separated by rounded projecting beads—that is, by *single* reeds—so that glancing sunlight reflects highlights above as well as shadows below, an effect that can change minute by minute, all around the building.

If the Temple might be regarded as a giant piece of furniture, that would be quite appropriate. After all, according to David Willson, it was meant to be "an altar built for his [that is, His] name alone."

Furnishing the Temple

John Doan was the oldest of three talented brothers who joined the Children of Peace. John was the cabinetmaker who constructed the Ark that sits at the centre of the Temple; Mahlon, a maker of carriages; and Ebenezer, the master builder of the Temple itself. John was born in Bucks County, Pennsylvania, on October 3, 1768. His granddaughter recorded that "he distinctly remembered the battle of Trenton, December 26, 1776... [and] seeing Washington's army encamped for a day and night upon the farm adjacent to that upon which his parents were living. At the proper age he was placed as an apprentice to learn the trade of a carpenter... He often spoke of having assisted in the erection of buildings in Philadelphia as well as in the country."

The Doans moved to Sharon in 1818, where John made his living making furniture. Surviving pieces of fine cabinetmaking attributed to Doan are simple in form yet unusually well crafted and detailed to take maximum advantage of the texture and grain of the wood. The Altar he built for the Temple was said to have taken exactly 365 days to complete, and it marked the completion of the seventh year of construction, in emulation of Solomon's Temple in Jerusalem.

In 1990, almost 160 years after it was sealed, restoration work on the Altar/Ark revealed a treasure trove of material. Cleverly hidden in a secret compartment was a "time capsule" — a history of the early years of the sect written by David Willson. The documents included a detailed description of their dispute with the Quakers, the effects of the War of 1812, their appeals to higher bodies in New York and Philadelphia and texts of the visions which led Willson to (re-)construct Solomon's Temple.

The Temple originally contained over three hundred distinctive "Temple chairs." Each member paid a fee for his or her chair — £1 for men, 10 shillings for women. The names of many members can still be found under the seats of the remaining 35 chairs. In recent years the museum has established a fund-raising

project based on these surviving chairs. To recognize a significant donation, a reproduction chair, carefully crafted following the pattern of the originals and bearing the name of each museum "Patron," will take its own place on the tiered floor of the Temple.

The oldest marked graves in the Children of Peace Burial Ground at the southern limits of the village date from 1820, though oral tradition puts the burial ground in use as early as 1818. This original cemetery was about 25 rods in size, or 82½ feet square.

As with all their rituals, the funerals of the Children of Peace were distinctive, a unique blend of their Quaker past with their innovative processions and musical skills. While David Willson's own funeral was the largest ever held in Sharon, it was probably typical, though diarist Amos Hughes recorded only the "programmed" part of the service. After reading the 23rd Psalm, "The Lord is my shepherd," the gathering intoned a hymn from Willson's most noted book, *Impressions of the Mind*. Later, they sang another hymn, "Preparations for Death," followed by a memorial and prayer by Abraham Doan. At the graveside, a final hymn: "A Call From the Tomb."

The burying ground

The burial ground expanded in 1878 when Jacob Lundy and his wife Hannah sold the northwest corner of Lot 6, Concession 3 to the Trustees of the Children of Peace for $73. By this time, however, the membership of the congregation had dropped precipitously; most of the newly purchased land went unused. The cemetery was then opened to nonmembers of the Children of Peace, who placed their graves along the south east fence-line and oriented their stones east-west; the Children of Peace stones are all oriented north-south.

After the Children of Peace disbanded in 1889, the care of the cemetery was left in the hands of David's grandson Absalom, who also owned the disused Temple and the meeting houses. In May 1912, when Absalom Willson and Charles E. Lundy invited tenders for the lumber of the Second Meeting House, they declared, "It is our intention to place ... a sum out of the proceeds sufficient to ensure the proper maintenance of the burying ground where lie the honoured remains of the founders and builders of this unique place of worship."

The last burial in the cemetery took place in 1935, and the cemetery was officially closed. Volunteers have continued to maintain the property since, incorporating as the Historic Sharon Burying Ground Association in 1952. The Burying Ground became a designated historic site in 1993.

From "Hope" to "Sharon"

After months in jail after the events of 1837, the "rebels" of Hope gained their release and returned home to their families. But the rancour within the divided group was such that the Children of Peace took their "Book of Sacred Record" and destroyed the pages dated after the Rebellion; they had "beaten one another with harsh words until the church was bleeding with the wounds." Seeking a rebirth, they changed the name of the village from "Hope" to "Sharon," and reorganized as the "Sharon Association."

In the following decade of relative calm and good fortune the congregation and community prospered. The village of Sharon reached its apogee in 1851. The local co-operative economy, with its concern for charity and the equal prosperity of all, had made the Children of Peace the most prosperous agricultural community in the entire province. Substantial farmhouses now dotted the surrounding landscape. Their political influence reached its peak, built upon deep, long-standing ties to both Baldwin and LaFontaine. Yet age was taking its toll on the village's patriarch, David Willson, now in his seventies. He could no doubt look back with pride at the accomplishments of a lifetime. But he would also have recognized that the religious community now generally known by his name, the "Davidites," would pass with him. He remained their only minister until his death in 1866.

His son John David took up leadership of the Children of Peace, reading his father's sermons to the aging and dwindling congregation. Ministers

from other denominations were gradually invited to preach in their meeting houses. In 1876, the group re-incorporated as a "charitable society." Finally, in 1889, after the death or departure of

Willson's sons, the Children of Peace faded away. The Temple and the other meeting houses fell into disrepair.

After decades of abandonment and the dismantling of parts of the complex, the York Pioneer and Historical Society purchased part of the original David Willson property in 1918, rescuing the Temple and its site along with other pieces of the material legacy of Children of Peace. This was among the earliest instances of historic preservation in Canada, and remarkable as an achievement of a group of citizens rather than any government. For much of the century, the YPHS maintained the Temple as a museum to the Children of Peace and to the local community.

The museum years

Though the "Davidites" had faded away as an organized group, their Temple still attracted national eyes. A noted member of the York Pioneers was Prime Minister Mackenzie King, grandson of William Lyon Mackenzie. After Mackenzie King gave a speech in the Temple in 1922, the minutes of the day reported that he

> received a cable from the English Premier, Mr. Lloyd George, asking if he would support the latter in repelling the Turks from Constantinople. He replied on the spot that the Canadian Parliament must decide on such a question. This reply, in the opinion of the English statesman, averted a second world war. Here the interesting fact emerges that in the Sharon Temple, that shrine of the Children of Peace, we may celebrate a great world decision for peace made by a York Pioneer.

The "museum years" began in 1918, but though it is now the members of the Sharon Temple Museum Society rather than the York Pioneer and Historical Society who care for the site, the legacy of the YPHS remains intact, in the landscape of the place, in the rescued artifacts and structures that make up the entire site, and in a lot of the knowledge we now have about the Children of Peace. One of the explicit reasons for the recognition of the Sharon Temple as a national historic site was the literally pioneering role of the YPHS in taking ownership of the historic place, decades before any government even thought it might be good to have any heritage at all.

Those who have studied its history have developed a strong sense that the Temple's ideals have modern resonance. In 1984, the University of Toronto organized a scholarly gathering, "The Sharon Temple and the Children of Peace," with historians, poets, musicologists and noted scholars that included J. M. S. Careless, Northrop Frye, Al Purdy and British architect Peter Smithson. At its conclusion, George Ignatieff, then-Chancellor of the University of Toronto and Canadian Ambassador for Nuclear Disarmament, declared:

> The architecture of the Temple, the music and the thoughts of the founder, David Willson, all remind us that life is a unified whole. The Children of Peace were witnesses to the conviction that co-operative relationships among Christians and Jews and men and women are our natural state. Conflict and enmity are aberrations and obstacles to be overcome. The sect created by these nineteenth century witnesses to the hope that all peoples could live in peace failed to survive. The hope itself and the ideas which inspired the Children of Peace live on and it is our challenge to see that they do not die... the spirit of David Willson and the Children of Peace lives on. In the age of the nuclear bomb we must all become children of peace if we hope to survive. This is not a perfectionist option for Utopian minorities. It is an urgent requirement for all of us and especially for our children.

Maintaining the legacy

The Temple and its site require constant attention to their upkeep. Since 1919, that care has been managed through innumerable private efforts and donations under the custody of the York Pioneer and Historical Society and, since 1991, the Sharon Temple Museum Society. The site is a "national historic site" by virtue of federal recognition, but it remains owned by its membership. Governments have provided modest assistance to operating costs from their own limited resources, and some large-scale restoration work has benefited from public grants.

A modest program of ongoing restoration and repair work is always in progress. The most recent larger-scale work was carried out in the mid- to late 1990s. Going further back in time there were also spurts of intensive maintenance and modest renewal in the late 1970s, the middle 1960s, the early 1950s, the early 1920s and at unknown intervals during the active years of the Children of Peace, from the 1830s into the 1870s.

1930

AUTHENTICITY

It is conventional for interpreters of historic sites to point out — proudly — what is original, or antique, or "genuine," or otherwise noteworthy. Anything not called to attention this way may be old, new, repaired or not at all historic. For the Temple, the entirety of the building is indeed "original, authentic, genuine and antique" at the very least, with the following *exceptions*, which are the result of the normal cycle of age, decay and modest repair.

This is the reality of old places: there are modest repairs and slight scars or abrasions, mostly healed, but visible to the critical eye. Visitors should keep in mind that this is among the very oldest buildings in the region — although, as a matter of interest, the Yonge Street Quaker meeting house of 1810, from which the Children of Peace were disowned still stands.

FROM THE TOP DOWN, AND THE OUTSIDE IN

The golden ball of peace suspended by chains at the topmost level has been restored (in 1996, for at least the second time) on its old armature of iron rods, and regilded. The roof, after accumulating several layers of wood and shingles in the 20th century, was reconstituted in the 1990s almost as it was originally built, but with cedar shingles instead of pine because the age, toughness and longevity of the local pine that covered the original can no longer be found except in old-growth forests thousands of miles away. The "restored" roofing project replaced very elegant but minimal concealed metal flashing with rather more modern comprehensive (still very much concealed) metal flashing. The exterior of the building has been repainted periodically, though for long periods there was very little paint on the walls. The windows have all been repaired in recent years so that they operate as they did originally, many having been painted shut for decades. Most of the glazing is not 170 years old, but it is impossible to say which pane is which.

The heavy timber sill beam around the perimeter just above the ground was replaced, in pieces, around 1977; the original mortise-and-tenon joints are now held together by steel angles and bolts. The steps outside each door are all replacements, and quite likely not the first replacements. The reconstruction of the perimeter fence, evident in period photographs, is under consideration.

2005

Inside, the joists beneath some parts of the flooring have been repaired. In some places, the noticeable slope in the floor will require correcting at some point. Many years ago, Jacob's Ladder was pushed a few inches westward for stiffening and strength. The interior has been repainted perhaps twice. Some small areas of plaster have had to be replastered. There are a couple of electrical outlets, neither old nor recent.

At the very centre of the space, the Altar, or Ark, had its windows reglazed in the early 1990s in a manner true to the evidence of old photographs. Its five spiked finials are inauthentic placeholders, standing in for five oil lamps. Its twelve small feet are reproductions, true to old photographs, since all but five of the originals had disappeared over time. The Altar/Ark has always been at the very centre, except for a temporary move, which revealed that the flooring beneath bore signs of wear like much of the rest of the floor: that still perplexes us.

There are also "modern" requirements for public access and public safety that require attention. But while the Temple also shows other signs of age that have not yet been attended to, what you see today is closer to its 19th-century aspect than it had been for much of the 20th.

For now, and for the future

In 1991 the charitable, not-for-profit Sharon Temple Museum Society assumed the obligations of the York Pioneer and Historical Society, and has owned and maintained the site and its legacy of buildings, artifacts and documents ever since. Its membership and Board of Directors have included local residents and business people, descendants of the founding families, representatives of the East Gwillimbury town council and the YPHS, heritage-minded advocates from the wider region and, it must be disclosed, the authors of this book.

Though recognized and marked as a provincial

1916

historic site in 1957, and as a national historic site in 1993, the Sharon Temple site has always remained in the ownership and care of that membership and a corps of dedicated volunteers, with management from season to season by a handful of skilled and astonishingly devoted workers who tend to the museum collections, structures and landscapes, and to its visitors.

Simply maintaining the material inheritance from the Children of Peace and keeping the forces of passing time at bay has been a constant struggle ever since its builders left the buildings for the last time. If mere survival after almost ninety years as a "heritage site" can be judged a modest success, then the rescue of the Sharon Temple after 1917 has proven the YPHS was right to have risked the venture. But mere survival is still hard work.

The Temple has had its strokes of added success in the past, but these almost always prove hard to sustain. In living memory, the summer festival "Music at Sharon" of the 1980s brought national profile to the Temple's extraordinary visual and sonic qualities, but the growth of the music audience strained the capacities and the floorboards of the place to its limits. The great idea — and it still is a great idea — to stage performances for the material benefit of the historic place *in that place* started as a modest success, but as the audiences expanded, so did the strains. The 1990 season of the Music at Sharon festival, the last at the Temple itself, commissioned the operetta *Serinette* by Harry Somers and James Reaney, an inventive and exciting staging of music and environmental theatre which played inside and all around the Temple, culminating, as the sun set, in the performance of an Illumination.

But festival performances could not produce enough revenue to expand the facilities of the place to accommodate the larger numbers of visitors and audiences, and so the Temple went quiet for a time. Eventually, performance schedules reappeared with more modest ambition, and perhaps the music that now resounds in the Temple might be considered far more precious.

1918

Meanwhile, this national historic site – the frontage of the farmland of its founding families two centuries ago – lies in the path of an inexorably encroaching suburban terrain. Its future, whether as tourist attraction or performance venue or educational resource or gathering place or good neighbour, will depend on both an accommodating new landscape and a conscientious new membership.

For now, the future plan might best be just to change "or" in the previous sentence to "and."

The demands of preserving historic places are unrelenting. Sustaining a viable and genuine connection with the past requires the ongoing maintenance of the material resources, along with public education and research. So the Temple and its site is ever in the midst of the program of repair and restoration that began in 1918 and renewed in 1991. The uneven pace depends on intermittent and generally limited funding, and in response to the occasional unhappy surprise typical to old places. It is not expected that this work will ever be finished.

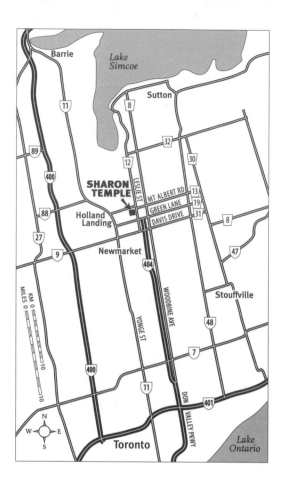

Mark Fram is an architecturally trained planner and designer, a scholar and instructor at the University of Toronto and a consultant in historic preservation. He is the author of *Well-Preserved: the Ontario Heritage Foundation's Manual of Principles and Practice for Architectural Conservation* (3rd ed., Boston Mills Press, 2003), and, among other projects, a forthcoming book on the architectural histories of the Temple at Sharon.

Albert Schrauwers is a professor of anthropology at York University and the author of *Awaiting the Millennium: the Children of Peace and the Village of Hope, 1812-1889* (University of Toronto Press, 1993). He is currently writing a volume on the role of the Children of Peace in promoting democracy and social justice in early Ontario.

Designed and typeset by Mark Fram

Printed and bound in Canada, at the Coach House

Coach House Books
401 (rear) Huron Street, on bpNichol Lane
Toronto, Ontario M5S2G5

Fax: 416 977 1158   Phone: 416 979 2217

www.chbooks.com